**For
Valentino Buttignol**

&

to all those who love Valentine's Day

VALENTINE'S DAY IS ...

BY GAIL GIBBONS

Holiday House / New York

Library of Congress Cataloging-in-Publication Data
Gibbons, Gail.
Valentine's Day is— / by Gail Gibbons.
p. cm.
ISBN-10: 0-8234-1852-9
ISBN-13: 978-0-8234-1852-7
1. Valentine's Day—Juvenile literature. I. Title.

GT4925.G5 2005
394.2618—dc22

2005045985

ISBN-13: 978-0-8234-1852-7 (hardcover)
ISBN-13: 978-0-8234-2036-0 (paperback)

ISBN-10: 0-8234-1852-9 (hardcover)
ISBN-10: 0-8234-2036-1 (paperback)

VALENTINE'S DAY IS...A CELEBRATION OF FRIENDSHIP AND LOVE.

It is celebrated on February 14. This special day grew out of old beliefs and customs.

In ancient Rome, people celebrated the beginning of spring with a festival. Boys picked names of girls from an urn to find their partners for the event. Often, the people they chose became their sweethearts.

Doves were a symbol of love.

VALENTINE'S DAY IS...SAINT VALENTINE.

About eighteen hundred years ago a kind man named Valentine was put in jail because of his religious beliefs. There are many stories about Valentine. In one he became friends with his jail guard, who had a blind daughter. Before Valentine died, he gave the guard a message to bring to the girl.

When the jail guard's daughter opened the message, she could see! The message read, "From your Valentine." Valentine died on February 14. Later he was named a saint.

VALENTINE'S DAY IS...POEMS.

It is believed that about six hundred years ago a French nobleman, the Duke of Orleans, was the first person to make valentines. While he was in prison, he wrote many love poems to his wife. Some poems mentioned Saint Valentine, who by then had become the patron saint of love.

VALENTINE'S DAY HAS MANY SYMBOLS.
VALENTINE'S DAY IS...HEARTS...

Red hearts have been a symbol of love since ancient times. A red heart is the most popular valentine symbol.

To give a heart is a symbol of giving the most important part of
yourself.

RIBBONS...

Often, ribbons are used to decorate valentines. The symbol of ribbons comes from the Middle Ages. When knights competed in tournaments, their sweethearts often gave them ribbons for good luck.

AND LACE.

Lace is often used to decorate valentines, too. The word *lace* comes from the Latin word *laqueus*. This word means "to snare or net," as in catching someone's heart.

VALENTINE'S DAY IS...CUPID!

Cupid was the god of love in ancient Rome. People thought that when Cupid shot one of his special arrows into someone's heart, the person fell in love. This is why he is a symbol of love.

VALENTINE'S DAY IS...VALENTINE CARDS.

I LOVE YOU!

You're divine, my Valentine!

HEARTS AND FLOWERS.

Some people save old valentines.

JUST A LITTLE VALENTINE

The Two of Us!

ROSES ARE RED,

On Valentine's Day, everyone likes receiving valentine cards. There are many different kinds. Some are fancy and have love poems or sayings in them.

Other valentine cards make you laugh. They can be silly.

Some valentine cards pop up when you open them. Others have moving parts. Still others actually have voices that say "Be my valentine" when the cards are opened.

Many people like to make their own valentines. If the card is not signed, it may keep a sweetheart guessing who sent the secret valentine.

Lots of people buy their valentine cards. There are so many different kinds to choose from.

VALENTINE'S DAY IS...
GIVING VALENTINES, TOO.

People give valentines to friends and loved ones. Some people even give valentines to their pets. Valentine cards may be sent far away.

VALENTINE'S DAY IS...FLOWERS AND...

People give flowers to the people they care about. The red rose is the flower of love.

CANDY.

Some people give candy, because it is sweet...to a sweetheart.
There are heart-shaped boxes full of chocolates. Other candies
are heart shaped and have messages on them.

VALENTINE'S DAY IS...
VALENTINE DECORATIONS.

There are red and pink hearts.

Cupids, lace, ribbons, and hearts are some of the things
that remind us of Valentine's Day.

VALENTINE'S DAY IS...
VALENTINE PARTIES...

People get together and have a good time.

TREATS AND GAMES.

There are lots of goodies to eat.

At school, classmates give each other valentine cards.

Some classmates may decorate a box. All the valentines are put in the box. Then the cards are taken out and distributed. Maybe this idea came from the time when the Romans picked names out of an urn.

Everyone gets lots of cards.

VALENTINE'S DAY IS...
A DAY OF GIVING AND SAYING...

"I LOVE YOU!"

HOW TO MAKE A VALENTINE

CUPIDS

PAPER LACE DOILY

RIBBONS

YOU NEED:

PAPER

CRAYONS and MARKERS

SCISSORS

GLUE

PHOTOS

STICKERS

GLITTER

1. Fold a piece of paper in half.

2. Draw half of a heart shape, starting at the fold.

3. Cut along the line.

4. Open the folded paper. Both halves of the heart will be equal.

5. Decorate the heart any way you want.

6. Write a special message on your valentine.